A Kalmus Classic Edition

Pablo de

SARASATE

(1844–1908)

SPANISH DANCE

Romanza Andaluza

Opus 22, No. 1

Urtext Edition

FOR VIOLIN AND PIANO

K 04366

A Kalmus Classic Edition

Pablo de

SARASATE

SPANISH DANCE

Romanza Andaluza

Opus 22, No. 1

Urtext Edition

FOR VIOLIN AND PIANO

K 04366

ROMANZA ANDALUZA

PAPLO DE SARASATE, OP. 22 Nº 1

K 4366

p
espressivo
p
B
f
dim.
mf
dim.
p
p
p
p

A Kalmus Classic Edition

Pablo de

SARASATE

(1844–1908)

SPANISH DANCE

Romanza Andaluza

Opus 22, No. 1

Urtext Edition

FOR VIOLIN AND PIANO

K 04366

cresc. - - poco - a - poco

6
appassionato
mf e molto espressione
p
p
f
mf
poco più lento
espressivo
D poco più lento
p
molto espressivo
p
poco rit.
poco rit.
Tempo I
mf
Tempo I
p

E poco animato
poco animato
p
f
f
presante
mf
F f
mf
f
4.

dim.
a tranquillo
G tranquillo
p
pp
H
p
tr
8
p
pp
p
pp

SARASATE

SPANISH DANCE

ISBN-10: 0-7579-2284-8
ISBN-13: 978-0-7579-2284-8

Alfred

alfred.com

K04366 $7.99 in USA

ISBN 0-7579-2284-8